Blends

sc

tw

blend

bl

ck

TWO SOUNDS

ft

cr

sm

YFG Kidz

Books, notebooks, journals, and more.
www.amazon.com/author/yfg-kidz

All images credited to Canva ®

What is a blend?

 two letters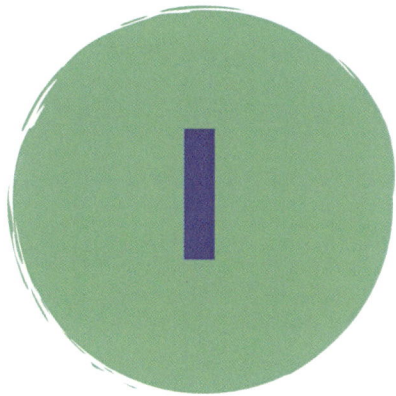

together

two sounds

b  l

Blends

l-blends

bl, cl, fl, gl, pl, and sl

★ Read and trace.

bl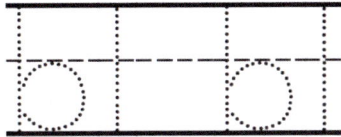

 blue

block

blink

blimp

blow

blend

black

blanket

blog

bloom

⭐ Read and trace.

cl

cl cl

clue

clap

click

clay

clip

cloud

clash

clock

climb

cliff

⭐ Read and trace.

fl   fl fl fl

 flag   flame

fly   floss

flat   flash

 flip   flower

flap   floor

Practice Blend /gl/ sound

⭐ Read and trace.

gl

gl gl

glad glide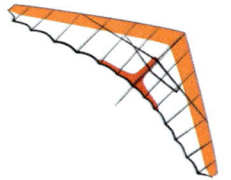

 glue glory

glow glass

globe gloat

glove glossy

Practice Blend /pl/ sound

⭐ Read and trace.

pl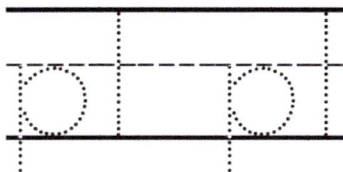

 play  plane

plug  plate

plan planet

plus plant

 plum please

Practice Blend /sl/ sound

⭐ Read and trace.

sl

s l | s l

 slice

 sleep

slide

slam

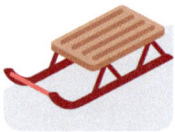 sled

slime

slim

slope

slop

slow

t-blends

tr, tw

Practice Blend /tr/ sound

⭐ Read and trace.

tr ─t̶r̶─ ─t̶r̶─

trip   truck

 trail   track

trap   trick

 treasure

triangle

⭐ Read and trace.

t**w**   tw tw

twig   twenty

twin   tweet

twirl   twice

 twist   twas

twitch   twelve **12**

r-blends

br, cr, dr, fr, gr, pr and tr

⭐ Read and trace.

br

br br

broom

brick

bread

brush

bridge

brown

⭐ Read and trace.

cr

cr cr

crow

cry

crab

cream

crush

cross

Practice Blend /dr/ sound

⭐ Read and trace.

dr

dr dr

drain

dress

drink

drum

drop

dragon

Practice Blend /fr/ sound

⭐ Read and trace.

fr

fr fr

frog

fruit

frame

frown

freeze

frisbee

⭐ Read and trace.

gr

grains

grapes

grass

grill

green

⭐ Read and trace.

pr

pr pr

price

prince

present

prune

prize

⭐ Read and trace.

tr   tr tr

 train

tree

tray

 treat

 trash

s-blends

sc, sk, sm, sn, sp, st, and sw

⭐ Read and trace.

sc

sc sc

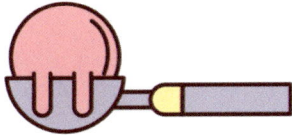

scoop

scream

scale

scarf

⭐ Read and trace.

sk

sk sk

skate

sky

skirt

skunk

⭐ Read and trace.

sm sm sm

smell

smile

smoke

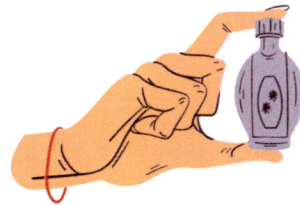

small

⭐ Read and trace.

sn   s n s n

snake

snail

snow

sneeze

⭐ Read and trace.

sp

sp   sp

spoon

speak

space

spin

⭐ Read and trace.

st

s t   s t

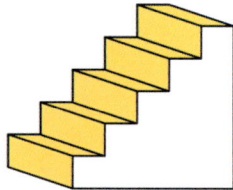

stair

stop

stick

star

⭐ Read and trace.

SW

sw sw

swing

swim

sweet

swan

ending blends

ft, lk, ld, lt, mp, nd, and nt

⭐ Read, trace, and match.

ft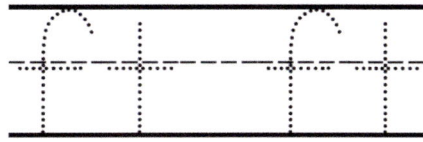

craft

gift

soft

lift

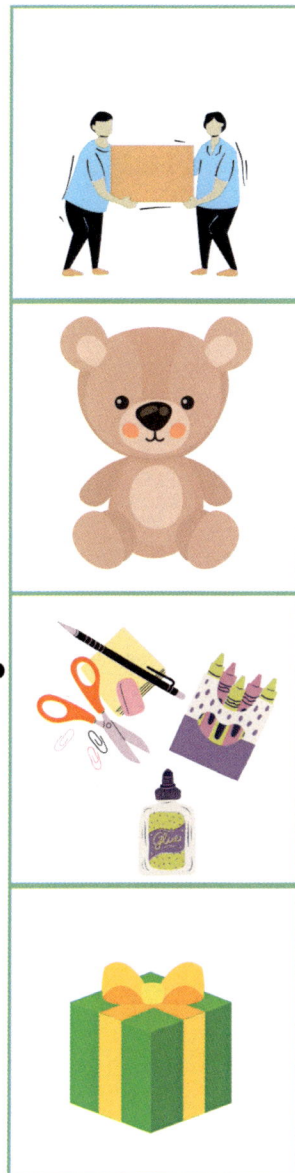

⭐ Read, trace, and match.

lk

lk lk

milk

chalk

talk

yolk

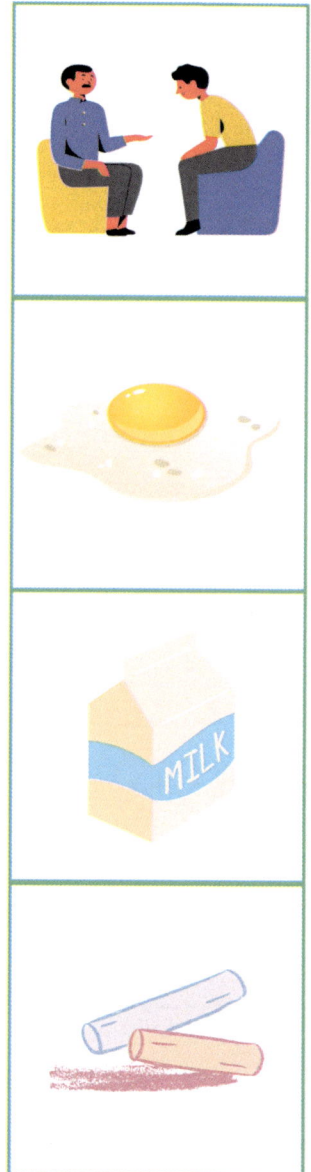

Practice Blend/ld/ sound

⭐ Read, trace, and match.

ld

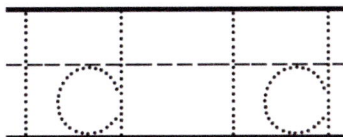

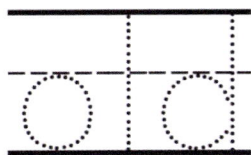

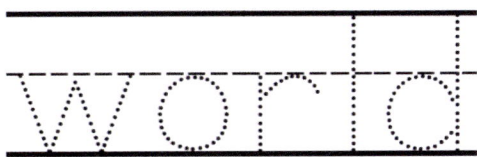

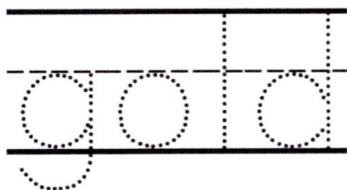

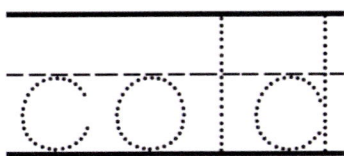

⭐ Read, trace, and match.

lt

belt

melt

bolt

salt

Practice Blend/mp/ sound

⭐ Read, trace, and match.

mp

mp mp

camp

lamp

stamp

jump

Practice Blend/nd/ sound

nd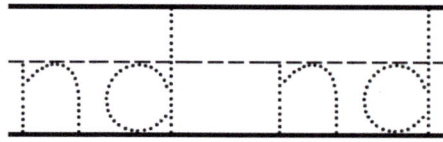

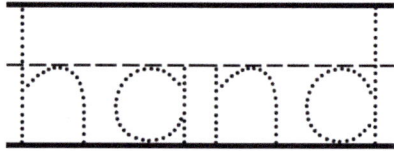

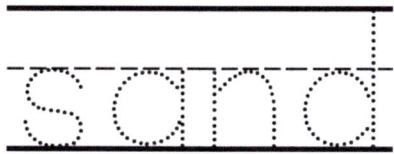

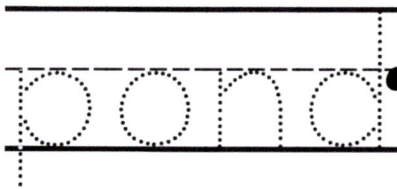

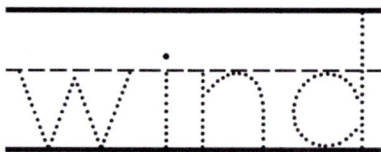

Practice Blend /nt/ sound

⭐ Read, trace, and match.

nt

nt nt

ant

pant

plant

tent

Certificate of Completion

Presented to

_____

- -

_____

Language Award

bl

tr

dr

nd

blend

bl

cr

tw

sk

cr

TWO SOUNDS

gl

sw

fr

sp

Made in the USA
Las Vegas, NV
18 September 2024